1

Village houses, Bridge Street

# Port Sunlight Village

## its history, buildings & houses

Illustrated by Pamela Blanchfield

Cover design Pamela Blanchfield

## Illustrations:

| | Page |
|---|---|
| Village houses Bridge Street | 2 |
| 19-23 Park Road by Douglas & Fordham 1892 | 7 |
| 11-17 Greendale Road by J J Talbot 1902 | 9 |
| The Gladstone Theatre & Lever House | 11 |
| Hulme Hall 1901 formerly a Museum & Art Gallery | 13 |
| The Lyceum, previously Park Rd. School & saddleback bridge over Dell | 15 |
| 38-52 Park Road by T M Lockwood 1893 | 17 |
| The Girls' Social Club now Port Sunlight Museum | 19 |
| The Lever Free Library 93-96 Greendale Road | 21 |
| The Bridge Inn & Victoria Bridge | 23 |
| The War Memorial by Sir William Goscombe John, R.A. 1921 | 25 |
| 15-27 Lower Road by Sir Charles H Reilly 1906 page | 27 |
| 1-3 The Causeway & 49 Greendale Road by Grayson & Ould 1901 | 28 |
| The Old Sun Dial, Bath Street | 29 |
| The Open Air Swimming Bath | 31 |
| The first village shop, 1891, later used as the Post Office | 32 |
| The Employees' Provident Society's Store | 33 |
| The Cottage Hospital, now the Leverhulme Hotel | 34 |
| The Village Fountain | 35 |
| The Technical Institute by J.J. Talbot 1903 | 37 |
| 19-22 Queen Mary's Drive by J Lomax-Simpson 1924 | 39 |
| The Band Stand by J Lomax-Simpson | 42 |
| Shakespeare Cottages by Edmund Kirby in 1896 | 43 |
| 2-4 Pool Bank & 26 Circular Drive by Grayson & Ould 1906 | 44 |
| 55-59 Corniche Road by Grayson & Ould 1899 | 45 |
| 1-9 Bridge Street & 26 Park Road by Douglas & Fordham 1893-4 | 46 |
| 17-21 Bolton Road by William Owen 1890 | 47 |

Port Sunlight village was created by William Hesketh Lever, later 1st Viscount Leverhulme. Born in 1851, he was the son of a Bolton grocer, and his innovative 'Sunlight Soap' brand launched his vision. He wanted to offer not only a better-quality product than what had been available before, but houses of a different kind, to improve the standard and happiness of the factory workers' lives.

The village was an experiment in ideal housing, and at the opening speech, Lever said: "It is my hope, my brother's hope … to build houses in which our work people will be able to live and be comfortable. Semi-detached houses, with gardens back and front in which they will be able to know more about the science of life than they can in a back slum, and in which they will learn that there is more enjoyment in life than in the mere going to and returning from work, and looking forward to Saturday night to draw their wages."

19-23 Park Road by Douglas & Fordham 1892

Begun in 1888 when Lever was only 38, the brand was swiftly expanded globally, along with the development of the village and shared amenities. Many Northern towns had very poor housing for workers, and he was unfaltering in his vision to create a much more beautiful environment.

His form of profit-sharing in his burgeoning business was to invest it in village facilities, for the enjoyment of all, thus enriching lives and offering pursuits of recreation otherwise very unlikely.

Completely different too was the public's view: they saw the fronts of houses with gardens, not squalid back yards as in other industrial towns.  It was an innovation when the cottages in Greendale Road were built facing the railway rather than the reverse.

11-17 Greendale Road by J J Talbot 1902

The houses are built in various architectural styles and no two groups of cottages are alike. William Owen, the Warrington architect built the factory as well as the first groups of houses. Many other nationally known architects submitted designs and later created more houses in the village.

The Rt. Hon. W E Gladstone, MP opened the eponymous Gladstone Hall in 1891. Gladstone Hall was the first assembly hall and recreational centre. It was also used as a men's dining room until a canteen was later proposed in the factory. The village council and other groups held meetings here, and Lever frequently lectured at Gladstone Hall, with sacred concerts being held on Sunday evenings.

The stage facilities were later improved and it is now used as a theatre by local music, dance and youth groups, as well as being visited over many years by a variety of famous artists, comedians and musicians.

The Gladstone Theatre & Lever House

In 1897 Birkenhead's May Queen visited Port Sunlight. She arrived on a wagonette drawn by three grey horses. Ever conscious of the quality of the children's lives, the day was made a special event by Mr and Mrs Lever. First there was a walk around the village, followed by a concert and tea party, with entertainment in the evening. Port Sunlight Brass Band played, and proceeds of £20. 14s. 7d went to Mr Thompson's Hemingford Street Mission which provided free meals for those in need, and is still in existence today.

The building of Hulme Hall followed, opened in 1901 and was named after Mrs Lever, Hulme being her maiden name. It was built as the girls' new restaurant, where up to 1,500 girls could obtain lunch at reasonable prices. Saturday evening dances were often held and Port Sunlight Philharmonic Society gave concerts here. For a time it was a Museum and Art Gallery and is now used for various functions.

Hulme Hall 1901 formerly a Museum & Art Gallery

Other buildings for shared use soon followed, such as the schools, one of which is now the Lyceum. The first village school was Park Road School built in 1896.  Sunday morning services and Sunday schools were held here before Christ Church was built.

In 1903 the second school, Church Drive was opened.  Park Road School was later called the Lyceum and became a staff-training college.  Before the Education Act 1902, the school was run by the Company and Mr and Mrs Lever took a keen interest in the children's welfare and education.

On the occasion of Queen Victoria's Diamond Jubilee in 1897, each child was given a bronze medallion to commemorate the Queen's long reign.  Led in procession through the village by Port Sunlight Prize Band, the children sang patriotic songs and waved Union Jacks.

The Lyceum, previously Park Road School & saddleback bridge over the Dell

The band was a source of much pride having come first the previous year in Birkenhead's Annual Brass Band Concert.  A Punch and Judy show, donkey rides, swings and races were organised on Jubilee day.  Mr and Mrs Lever awarded prizes before tea in Gladstone Hall.

Two young children, unaware of the competitive element of such things, ran a whole race holding hands.  As they were the only ones in the event, it was declared a dead heat much to everyone's amusement.

The saddleback bridge over the Dell was designed by Douglas and Fordham in 1894 and is based on the traditional packhorse bridge.

Lever and his family lived at Bridge Cottage situated by the Dell.  He was very much hands-on with the whole village and factory development.

38-52 Park Road by T M Lockwood 1893

By 1895 the factory had doubled in size, and by 1900 there were 400 houses in Port Sunlight.  The factory was finished in 1889 and the site provided ready means of transporting goods with the railway on one side and the River Mersey on the other.

The outside design of Lever House was classically inspired.  The clock over the doorway is five feet in diameter above which are the Royal Arms.  The remainder is built in red Ruabon brick in character with the factory.

In 1913, the Girls' Club opened in the Diamond and was a special interest of Lady Lever.  They had reading and poetry circles, rambles and instruction in home craft.

Designed by James Lomax-Simpson, the building is on King George's Drive, and is now Port Sunlight Museum.

The Girls' Social Club now Port Sunlight Museum

Port Sunlight Museum lies close to the art gallery and today has a shop, runs informative village walking tours, as well as offering an opportunity to learn how life used to be lived, which can be seen by visiting a furnished 'Edwardian Worker's Cottage', open to the public.

Many different events are organised in the village throughout the year both for local people and up to 300,000 visitors.

Some very grand excursions of employees were organised: in 1900 1,600 went by train and boat to Paris, and in 1910, 2,200 went to Brussels. Port Sunlight Station opened in 1914, and was originally for the private use of the work people, only becoming a public station in 1927.

The building at 93 – 96 Greendale Road was formerly The Lever Free Library having originally been used as a Girls' Hostel for a short time.

The Lever Free Library, 93 – 96 Greendale Road

Bridge Inn is named after Victoria bridge which spanned a tidal inlet at this point. Opened in 1900, it is built in the style of an old English coaching house. Originally a 'temperance hotel' it was licensed a few years later as the result of a poll of village residents.

The village bandstand was built in 1907 at the north end of the Diamond, and later moved to the middle. It was in the Ionic style, and designed by J Lomax-Simpson. However, when this area was further developed and the rose garden created in 1932, it was demolished.

Shakespeare Cottages were designed by Edmund Kirby in 1896, and built at Poet's Corner. They were based on Shakespeare's birthplace. Constructed using old building methods such as wooden pegs, they unfortunately were not popular being very dark inside, and were later demolished in 1938.

The Bridge Inn & Victoria Bridge

Ernest Prestwich, a student at Liverpool School of Architecture won a competition in 1910 which was for a plan to design the remaining stage of the village's development. From his idea plans were created to form a north-south axis, the Diamond, with a central axis crossed by The Causeway. The War Memorial stands at the intersection and was planned from 1916 by Sir William Goscombe John and was unveiled in 1921.

At the base of the runic cross are figures symbolising Defence of the Home, eleven figures in all. The four large bronze groups on the parapet represent Naval, Military, Anti-Aircraft and Red Cross Services. The children in the group carry garlands and wreaths in memory of the fallen and represent hope for the future. Names of those who fought in both wars are engraved on bronze panels. A large wreath bears the words: "Their names shall remain forever and their glory shall not be blotted out".

The War Memorial by Sir William Goscombe John, R.A. 1921

The house-building continued right up to 1925, the year of Lord Leverhulme's death, and even beyond.  There was a gradual move away from Tudor styles as the village expanded.  A crescent of seven houses was designed in 1906 by C. H. Reilly of Liverpool on Lower Road.

Many other architects followed with eclectic architectural designs, such as Lever's friend Simpson and his son James Lomax-Simpson, Lockwood & Sons of Chester and Sir Charles Reilly of Liverpool.  These then included prominent London architects, including Sir Edwin Lutyens, Sir Ernest George and Maurice Bingham Adams.

Houses of different styles appeared, including some in the style of the Arts and Craft movement.  The work and flair of almost thirty architects made this beautiful garden village so varied and aesthetically appealing.

15-27 Lower Road by Sir Charles H Reilly 1906

1-3 The Causeway & 49 Greendale Road by Grayson & Ould 1901

The Old Sun Dial, Bath Street

Visually although the houses are different, all have lawns facing to the road. They differ in size internally, but almost all were built with bathrooms. As well as having a gas supply, in the 1920s the additional installation of electricity enabled the residents to enjoy a far better standard of living than many at this time.

Port Sunlight had its own village shop, open-air swimming pool, inn, a gymnasium, a cycling club, Boys' Brigade, choir, bowling green, tennis court, football field, rifle range and girls' and boys' recreational grounds, as well as an auditorium seating over 3,000.

Lord Leverhulme proved a partnership could exist between capitalism and the workers, and that "it would work for lasting good".

The Open Air Swimming Bath

The first village shop, 1891, later used as the Post Office

The Employees' Provident Society's Store

The Cottage Hospital, now the Leverhulme Hotel

The Village Fountain

There was great opportunity for recreation during free time. The bowling green and Pavilion were built in 1896. The latter was extended in 1968 and is now known as the Lever Club. The village also had its own cottage hospital, later a Nursing Home, which is now the Leverhulme Hotel and restaurant, on Lodge Lane. It also had its own fire service.

The Lady Lever Art Gallery, the Technical Institute and Christ Church were special gifts given to the people at Lever's own personal expense. Hesketh Hall, Boundary Road was originally The Technical Institute, designed by J.J. Talbot and completed 1903. After the First World War it became the headquarters of the Port Sunlight branch of the Royal British Legion until it closed in 2012. Later the building was carefully restored and preserved, with the sympathetic conversion to residential use of 14 apartments.

The Technical Institute by J.J. Talbot 1903

Christ Church is built in Gothic style of red Cheshire sandstone with a richly carved oak interior. After Lady Lever's death in 1913, a narthex was added at the west end to form a shrine to his wife. Later, Lord Leverhulme, his son and wife were also buried here.

Christ Church is non-denominational, and was designed in 1902-4 by Owen and his son, Segar.

The same firm designed the impressive, but very different, Lady Lever Art Gallery, a masterpiece of Beaux-Art Classical architecture. The foundation stone of the Lady Lever Art Gallery was laid in 1914 from Hulme Hall in a ceremony using remote control. King George V and Queen Mary pressed a button on a model and as they saw a miniature crane lower a stone, simultaneously the actual event took place.

19-22 Queen Mary's Drive by J Lomax-Simpson 1924

Situated at the end of the Diamond the gallery commemorated Elizabeth Ellen Hulme, Lady Lever. Married in 1874, his wife died in 1913, before her husband was raised to the peerage. As a result, Elizabeth was Lady Lever, but not Lady Leverhulme, hence the gallery's name. In 1906 Lever became M.P. for Wirral and in 1911 he was made a Baronet, and became known as Sir William Hesketh Lever. He became Baron in 1917 and adopted 'Hulme' into his title: Baron Leverhulme of Bolton-le-Moors, combining his wife's maiden name with his own, and was then known as Lord Leverhulme. In 1922 he was created a Viscount, becoming Viscount Leverhulme.

A connoisseur and avid collector on a grand scale, numerous beautiful items were personally chosen by Lord Leverhulme and gifted to the Lady Lever Art Gallery, including an outstanding collection of Pre-Raphaelite paintings, sculpture, porcelain, furniture and many other rare and fine objects d'art.

West of the art gallery is a monument to Lord Leverhulme, a tall, black obelisk which was designed by Lomax-Simpson in 1930, with further allegorical sculptures by Sir William Reid Dick. Christ Church has a specially added personal table monument, with effigies of Lord Leverhulme and his wife carved by Goscombe John, commissioned after his wife's death.

Most of the houses have since been modernised, and the company evolved to become later known as Unilever. From the 1980s some houses were sold and are now owned privately. Previously only those who worked for the company lived there. Since 1978 Port Sunlight was declared a designated Conservation Area containing over 900 Grade II listed buildings. Port Sunlight Village Trust, a charitable trust set up in 1999 by Unilever, owns about 300 houses and the income generated from letting these properties helps ensure facilities and the appearance of the village is well-maintained.

The Band Stand by J Lomax-Simpson

Shakespeare Cottages by Edmund Kirby in 1896

2-4 Pool Bank & 26 Circular Drive by Grayson & Ould 1906

55–59 Corniche Road by Grayson & Ould 1899

1-9 Bridge Street & 26 Park Road by Douglas & Fordham 1893-4

17-21 Bolton Road by William Owen 1890

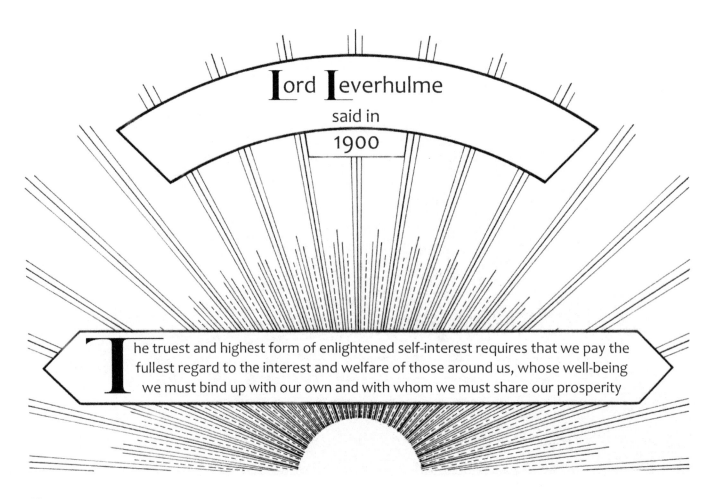

**Lord Leverhulme**

said in

1900

The truest and highest form of enlightened self-interest requires that we pay the fullest regard to the interest and welfare of those around us, whose well-being we must bind up with our own and with whom we must share our prosperity

Pamela Blanchfield

Born in Liverpool
the author, artist and poet has been involved in many creative fields

*Other books by Pamela Blanchfield:*

'"Why?" She Wondered' (for young people), ISBN: 978-1-3999-5170-8

'My Moon Sketch & Note Book' (for all age groups), ISBN: 978-1-3999-5171-5

'Horace the Hedgehog' (for children of all ages), ISBN: 978-1-3999-4440-3

'The Cats' Hotel' (15 cats' stories), ISBN: 978-1-3999-3415-2

'Show Me The Mountain Bright Meadows Below' (poetry, for adults), ISBN: 978-1-3999-2781-9

'Naked Love Tokens' (poetry, for adults), ISBN: 978-1-3999-4277-5

Printed in Great Britain
by Amazon

22614394R00031